Midwest

by Joanne Mattern

BELLWETHER MEDIA • MINNEAPOLIS, MN

Blastoff! Readers are carefully developed by literacy experts to build reading stamina and move students toward fluency by combining standards-based content with developmentally appropriate text.

LEVELS

Level 1 provides the most support through repetition of high-frequency words, light text, predictable sentence patterns, and strong visual support.

Level 2 offers early readers a bit more challenge through varied sentences, increased text load, and text-supportive special features.

Level 3 advances early-fluent readers toward fluency through increased text load, less reliance on photos, advancing concepts, longer sentences, and more complex special features.

★ **Blastoff! Universe**

Reading Level

Grade K

Grades 1–3

Grade 4

This edition first published in 2025 by Bellwether Media, Inc.

Library of Congress Cataloging-in-Publication Data

Names: Mattern, Joanne, 1963- author.
Title: Midwest / by Joanne Mattern.
Description: Minneapolis, MN : Bellwether Media, Inc., [2025] | Series: Blastoff! Readers : regions of the United States | Includes bibliographical references and index. | Audience: Ages 5-8 | Audience: Grades 2-3 | Summary: "Simple text and full-color photography introduce beginning readers to the Midwest. Developed by literacy experts for students in kindergarten through third grade"-- Provided by publisher.
Identifiers: LCCN 2024039227 (print) | LCCN 2024039228 (ebook) | ISBN 9798893042474 (library binding) | ISBN 9798893043440 (ebook)
Subjects: LCSH: Middle West--Juvenile literature.
Classification: LCC F351 .M346 2025 (print) | LCC F351 (ebook) | DDC 977--dc23/eng/20240910
LC record available at https://lccn.loc.gov/2024039227
LC ebook record available at https://lccn.loc.gov/2024039228

Editor: Kieran Downs Designer: Brittany McIntosh

Printed in the United States of America, North Mankato, MN.

Table of Contents

Welcome to the Midwest!

The Midwest is a region
of the United States.
The region includes 12 states.

The Midwest is sometimes called "America's Breadbasket." The area got that nickname because it produces so much grain.

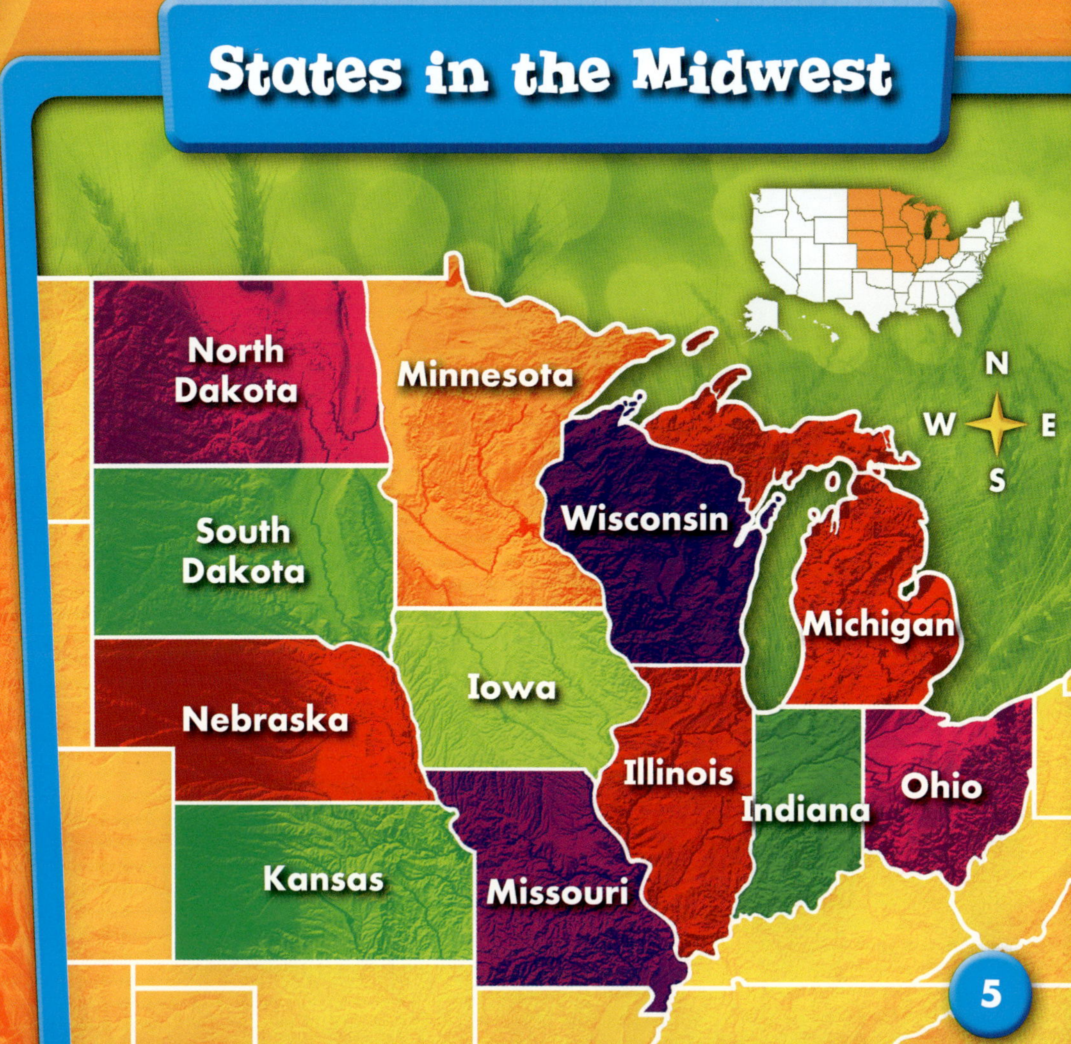

The Land, Weather, and Wildlife

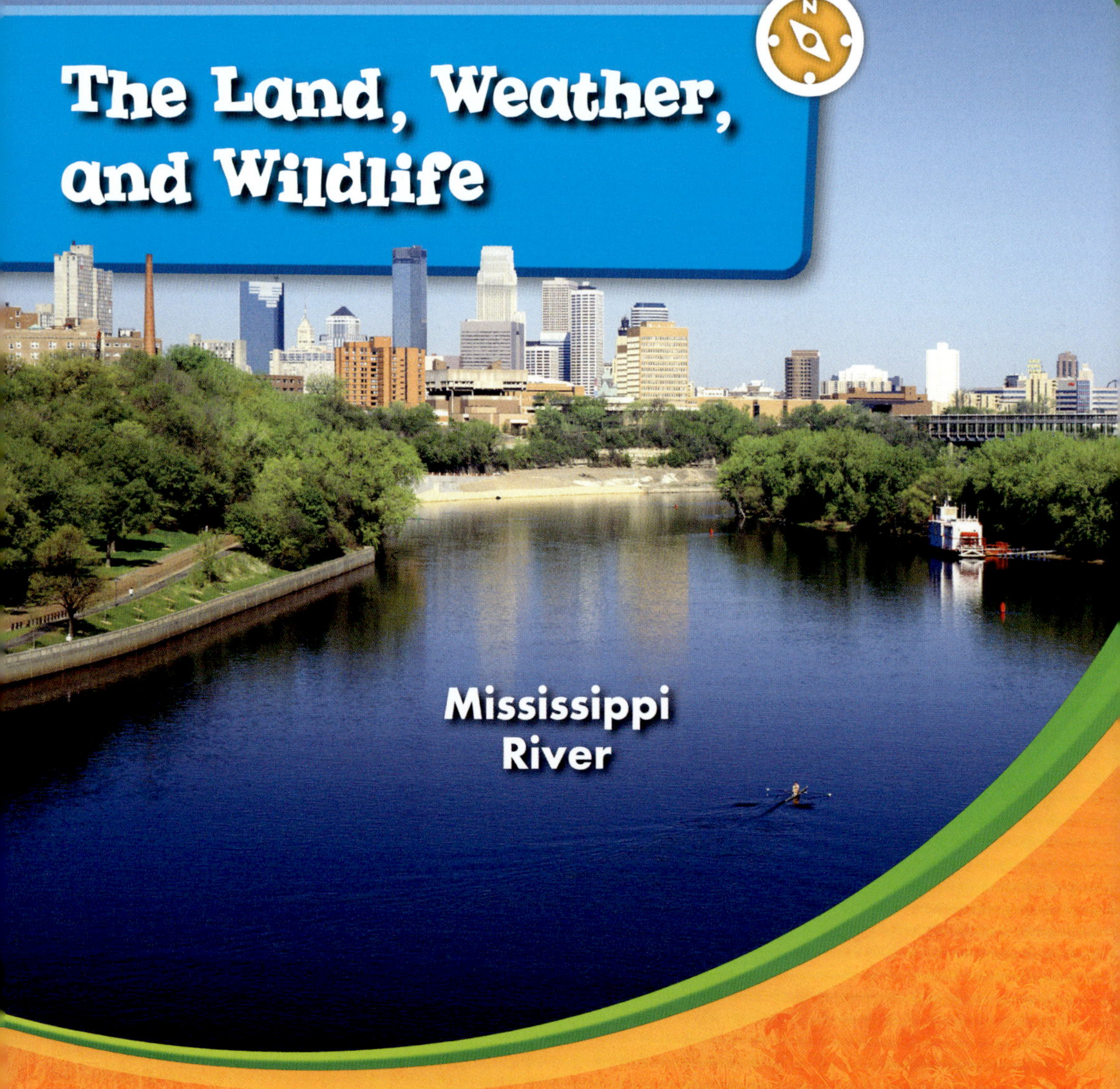

Mississippi River

Much of the Midwest is covered by the **Great Plains**. The land is mostly flat.

The Mississippi, Missouri, and Ohio are important rivers in the Midwest. Most of the **Great Lakes** are found in this region, too.

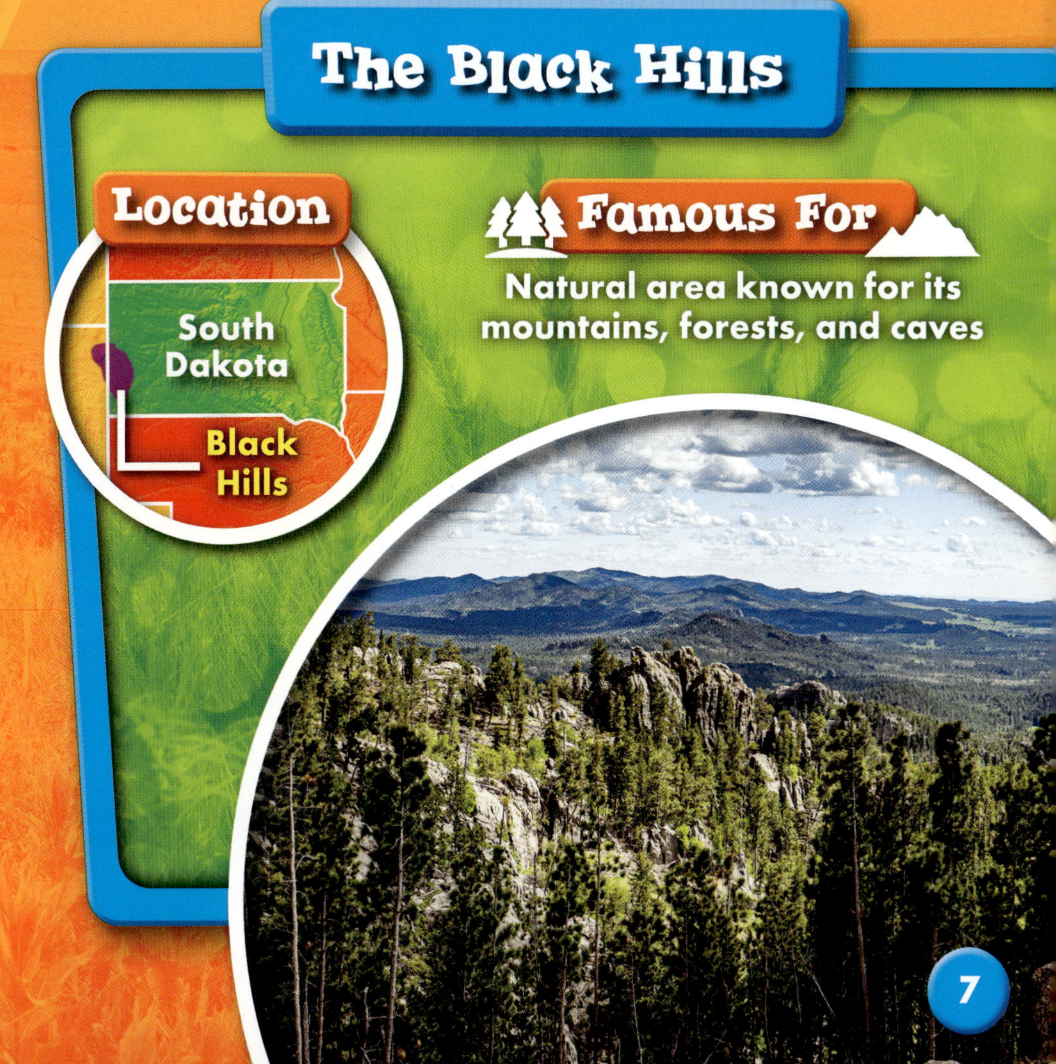

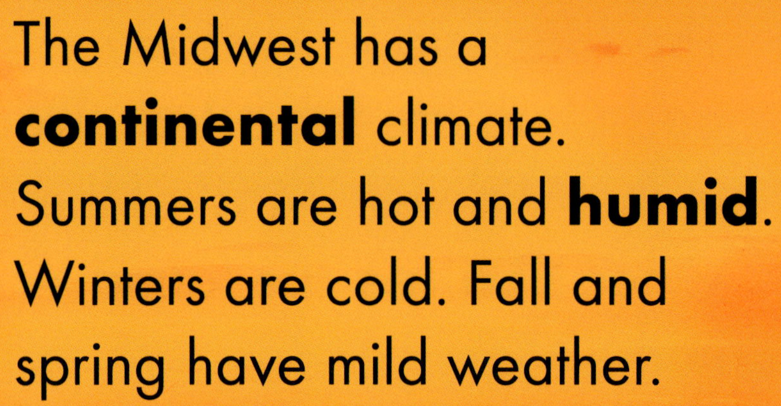

The Midwest has a **continental** climate. Summers are hot and **humid**. Winters are cold. Fall and spring have mild weather.

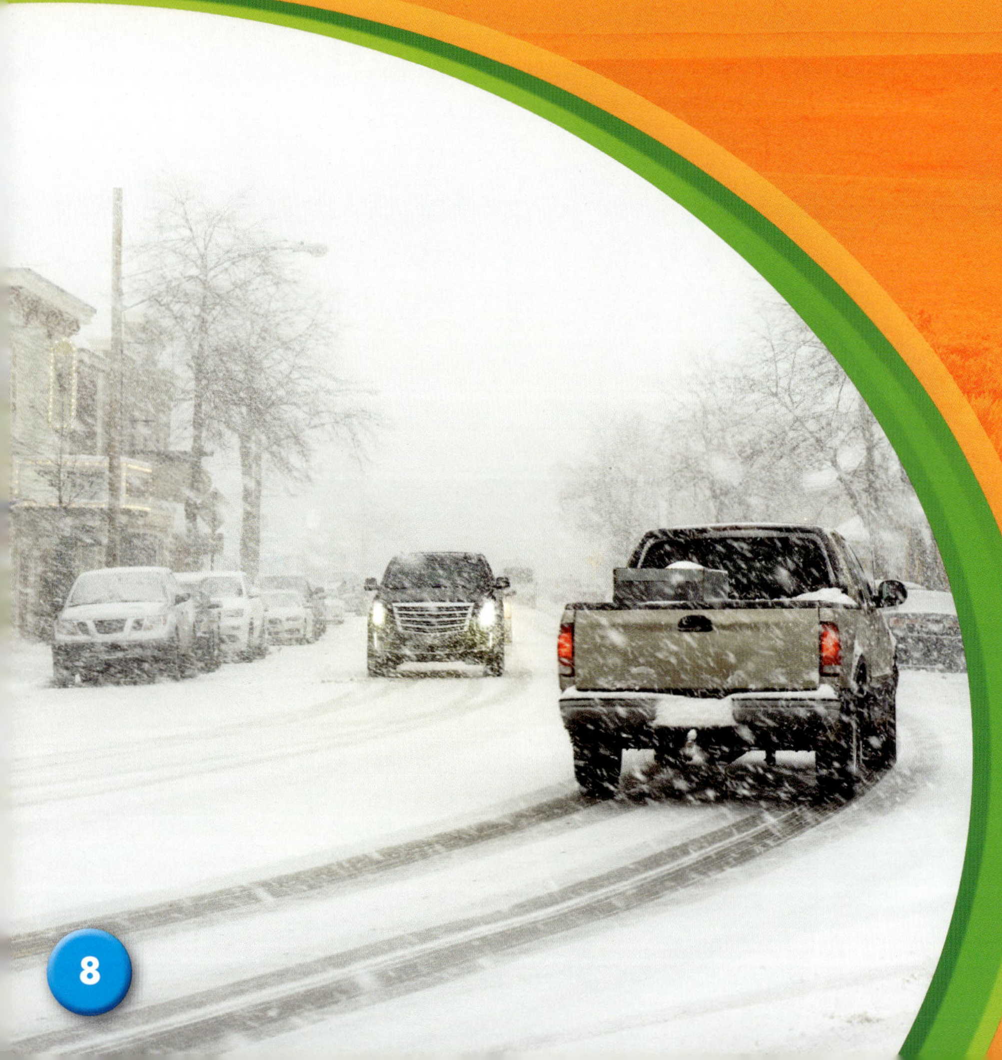

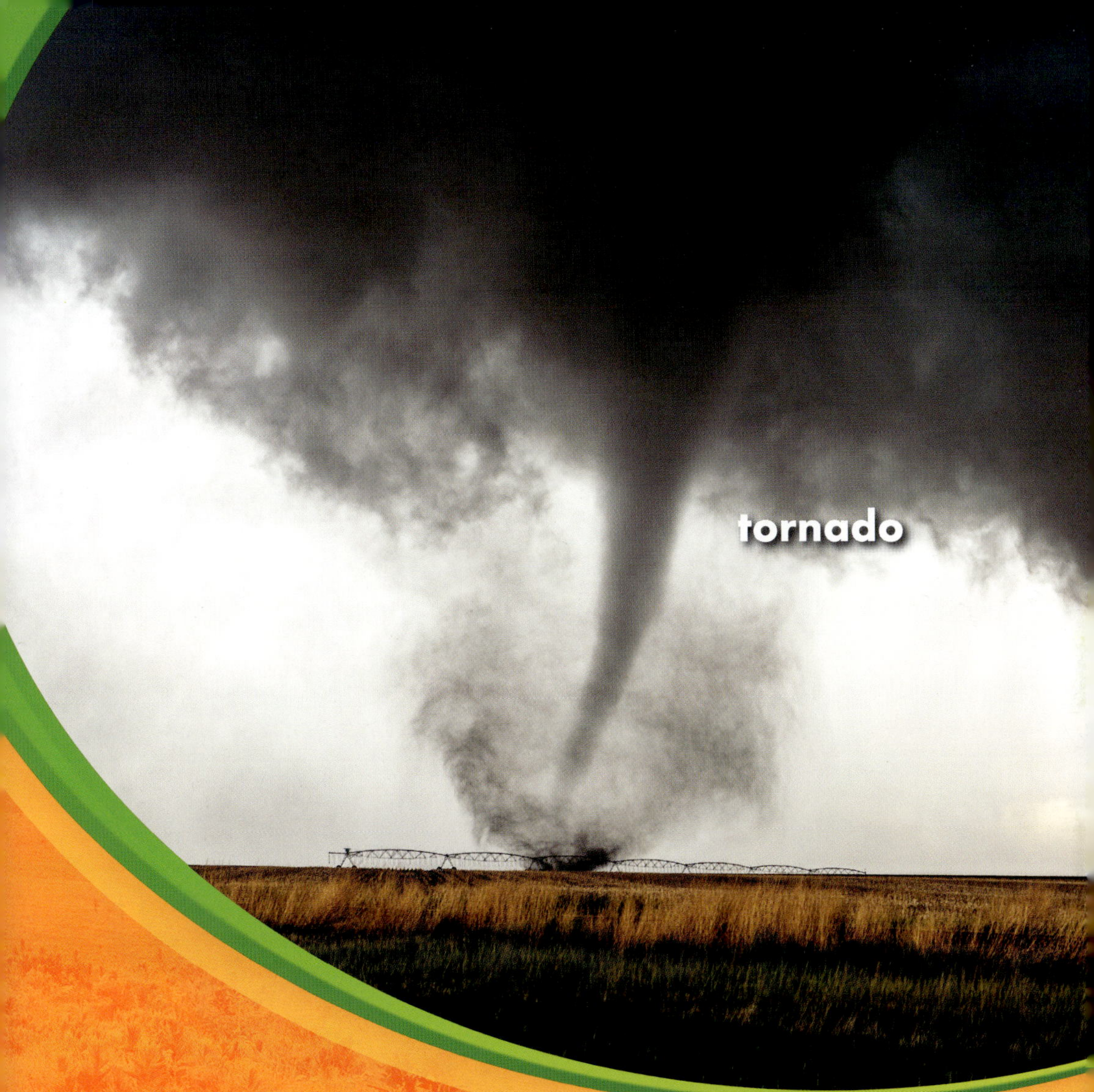

tornado

Thunderstorms and **tornadoes** happen in the spring and summer. Snow often falls in the winter.

Many animals live in the Midwest. Black bears live in northern forests. Beavers and muskrats swim in lakes and rivers.

Woodpeckers, bald eagles, and other birds fly in the Midwest's skies. Grouse hide in grasses.

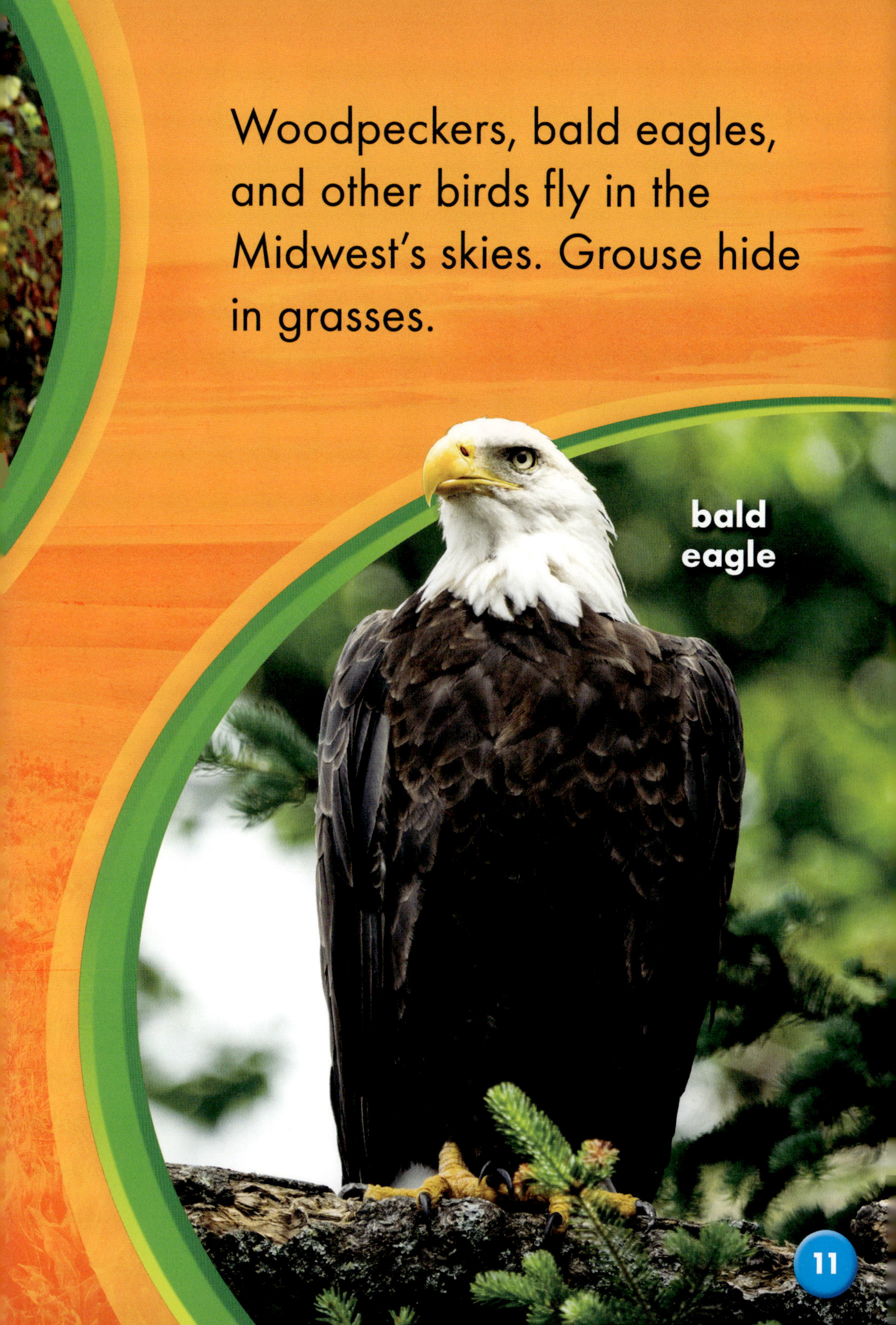

Natural Resources and Industry

Agriculture is an important **industry** in the Midwest. The area has plenty of fresh water. It also has **fertile** soil. These allow farmers to grow many crops.

Midwestern factories make cars, foods, and other products.

Resource to Industry

Agriculture

freshwater sources and fertile soil

many crops

People of the Midwest

Chicago, Illinois

Many Midwesterners have **ancestors** from Europe. Others may have African or Hispanic ancestors.

Most people in the Midwest live in **urban** areas. Chicago, Illinois, is the largest city in the region. Many other people live in **rural** areas.

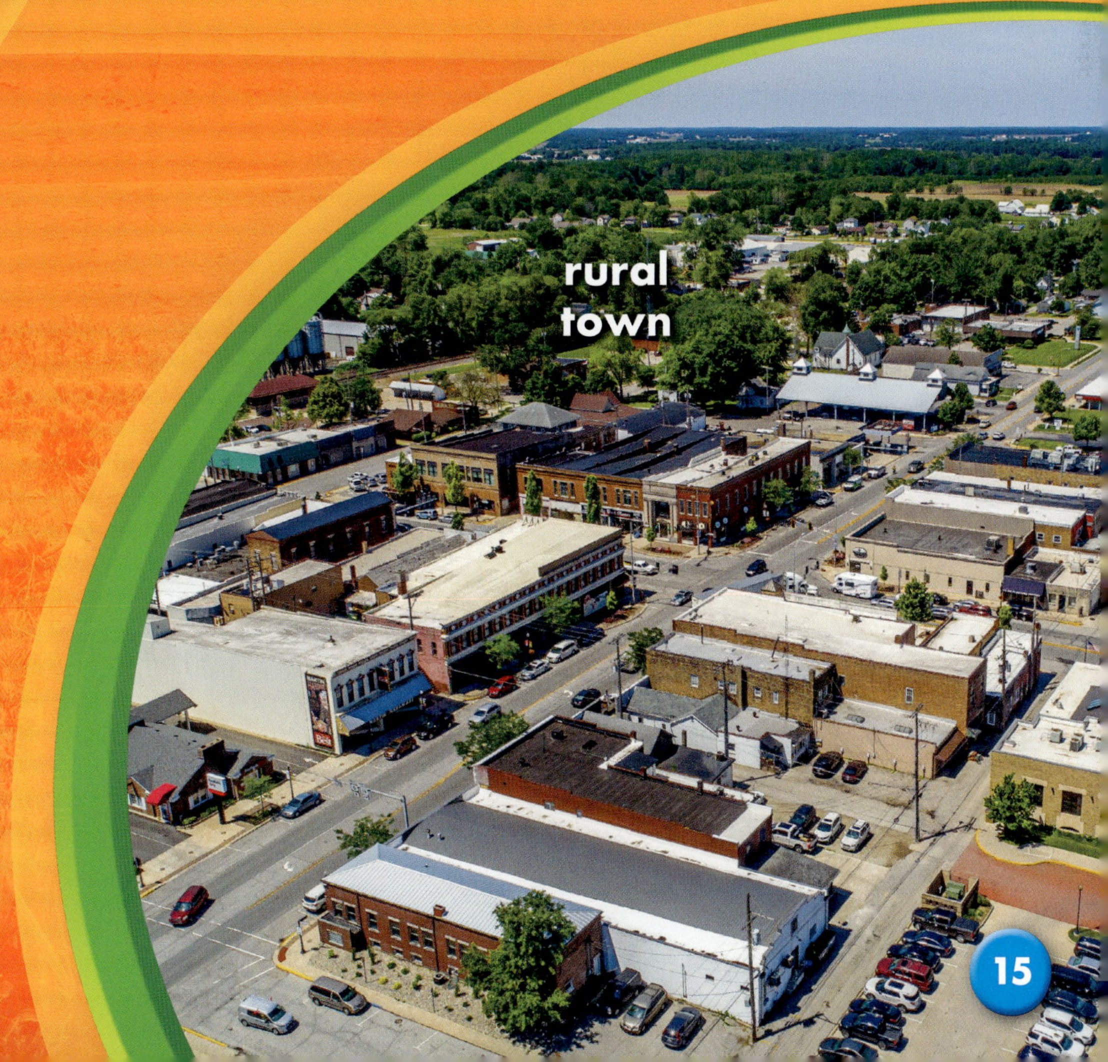

People in the Midwest enjoy **barbecue**. These slowly cooked meats include beef, chicken, and pork.

Many people eat fried cheese curds. Pierogies are another favorite. These bites of dough are filled with potatoes and onions.

People in the Midwest enjoy the outdoors. They hike, bike, and camp in forests and parks. They play many different sports.

People come together for state fairs. There is always a lot to do in this region!

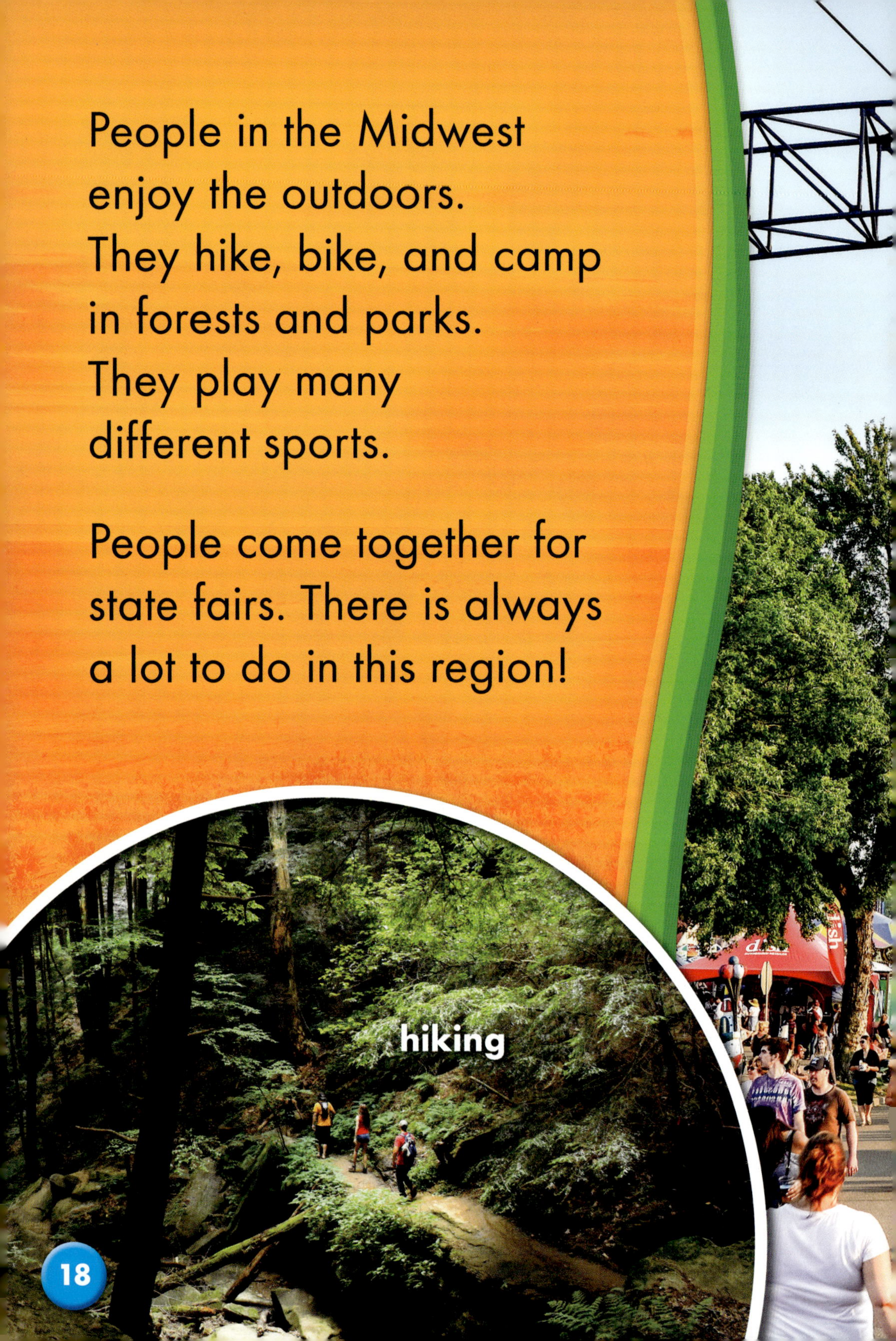

hiking

Places to Visit
N
W
E
S
Mount Rushmore
Keystone, South Dakota
Gateway Arch
St. Louis, Missouri
Bayard, Nebraska
Chimney Rock
Minnesota State Fair

Midwest Fast Facts

3 Largest Cities (2020)

1 **Chicago, Illinois**

Population: around 2.7 million

2 **Columbus, Ohio**

Population: 905,748

3 **Indianapolis, Indiana**

Population: 887,642

State Populations (2020)

North Dakota
779,094

Minnesota
5.7 million

South Dakota
886,667

Wisconsin
5.9 million

Michigan
10.1 million

Iowa
3.2 million

Nebraska
2 million

Illinois
12.8 million

Ohio
11.8 million

Kansas
2.9 million

Missouri
6.2 million

Indiana
6.8 million

Major Sports Teams

Chicago Cubs

(MLB)

Green Bay Packers

(NFL)

Indiana Pacers

(NBA)

Famous Face

Name: John Legend
Hometown: Springfield, Ohio
Famous for: Award-winning musician and actor

Smallest State

Indiana
36,420 square miles
(94,327 square kilometers)

Largest State

Michigan
96,713 square miles
(250,486 square kilometers)

Glossary

agriculture—the practice of raising crops and animals

ancestors—relatives who lived long ago

barbecue—food that is seasoned and slowly cooked over an open fire

continental—referring to a climate that has hot summers and cold winters

fertile—able to support growth

Great Lakes—large freshwater lakes on the border between Canada and the United States; the Great Lakes are Superior, Michigan, Ontario, Erie, and Huron.

Great Plains—a region of flat or gently rolling land in the central United States

humid—having a lot of water in the air

industry—a group of businesses that provide a certain product

rural—related to the countryside

tornadoes—funnel clouds that touch down on the ground

urban—related to cities or city life

To Learn More

AT THE LIBRARY

Jacobson, Bray. *The Mississippi River.* New York, N.Y.: Gareth Stevens, 2023.

Sabelko, Rebecca. *Chicago.* Minneapolis, Minn.: Bellwether Media, 2025.

Spanier, Kristine. *Explore the Midwest.* Minneapolis, Minn.: Jump!, 2023.

ON THE WEB

FACTSURFER

Factsurfer.com gives you a safe, fun way to find more information.

1. Go to www.factsurfer.com.
2. Enter "Midwest" into the search box and click 🔍.
3. Select your book cover to see a list of related content.

Index

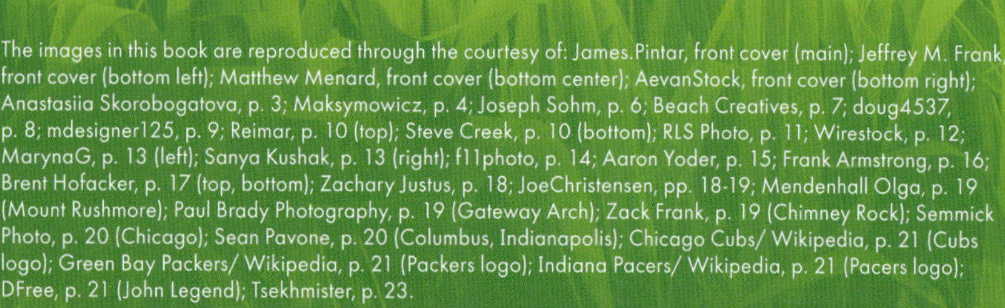
The images in this book are reproduced through the courtesy of: James.Pintar, front cover (main); Jeffrey M. Frank, front cover (bottom left); Matthew Menard, front cover (bottom center); AevanStock, front cover (bottom right); Anastasiia Skorobogatova, p. 3; Maksymowicz, p. 4; Joseph Sohm, p. 6; Beach Creatives, p. 7; doug4537, p. 8; mdesigner125, p. 9; Reimar, p. 10 (top); Steve Creek, p. 10 (bottom); RLS Photo, p. 11; Wirestock, p. 12; MarynaG, p. 13 (left); Sanya Kushak, p. 13 (right); f11photo, p. 14; Aaron Yoder, p. 15; Frank Armstrong, p. 16; Brent Hofacker, p. 17 (top, bottom); Zachary Justus, p. 18; JoeChristensen, pp. 18-19; Mendenhall Olga, p. 19 (Mount Rushmore); Paul Brady Photography, p. 19 (Gateway Arch); Zack Frank, p. 19 (Chimney Rock); Semmick Photo, p. 20 (Chicago); Sean Pavone, p. 20 (Columbus, Indianapolis); Chicago Cubs/ Wikipedia, p. 21 (Cubs logo); Green Bay Packers/ Wikipedia, p. 21 (Packers logo); Indiana Pacers/ Wikipedia, p. 21 (Pacers logo); DFree, p. 21 (John Legend); Tsekhmister, p. 23.